james brown is ~~dead~~

JAMES BROWN
IS ~~DEAD~~

and other poems

JIBADE-KHALIL HUFFMAN

TABLE OF CONTENTS

Voice-Over *Now That I Can Dance*

James Brown is Dead

Terrence Malick's Die Hard: With a Vengeance

Way Down East

Don't Tell Mom the Babysitter's Dead

Voice-Over *We Don't Need Another Hero*

VOICE-OVER
Now That I Can Dance

I like to masturbate to pictures of pregnant women. I write to television actors and people in movies and ask them for advice. I write to Oprah Winfrey and I ask her for a job. I ask Richard Roundtree to make me his personal assistant. I get a letter from one of Oprah's assistants saying that while Oprah appreciates my initiative she can do no better than offer me some of the products she has given away on the air. I live off the money I make at the restaurant and between the shift meal and selling a set of watches Oprah's assistant sends me I don't have to spend any money for the first six months we live in Florida.

I save what I make at the restaurant and I buy myself the complete first season of "Jake and the Fat Man" on DVD and stay up most of the night watching the first ten or so episodes and the next day I go to the store and I come back with ice cream and many kinds of chips. I take off my bra and put on slippers and sit at my desk and write a letter to the president of Party Metropolis, after I call, after I am, at various points, ignored and yelled at in the course of trying to get my money back for a product they insist I cannot return. Once they hang up on me and I call back and curse out the woman who'd hung up on me.

In my letter to the president of the company, I write about my mother's commitment to making the best product that you can make. I write down some of her favorite sayings, I write down the one about animal cruelty and how it could be prevented by corporations issuing full refunds to consumers who wish to return a strobe light and disco ball-combination. I write down another one of her favorite sayings and then I dedicate a whole paragraph to my favorite, to the one about calling again and calling again as a means of sustaining the conversation.

We are in my room, in the bedroom I converted into an office, when we hear CBS has exploded, over the radio, after I am the one-hundredth caller in the race for tickets to see Johnny Mathis. All of the other networks are running the footage over and over and running the commentary of a leading expert.

"This is the end of history as we know it. This had to happen, this could have been prevented with a more concerted effort from everyone in the community."

Another commentator passes out on the air, so flustered by the catastrophe that he cannot continue speaking and barely manages to sign off before he goes under, when they still have five minutes before they are supposed to go to commercial.

I put on a pair of sweatpants over the cheerleading outfit I was wearing to make fun of you and your desires. I turn off the television, and you put on a recording of a jailbreak on the tape deck and we make out and fall asleep.

This is what I sound like on the radio first thing in the morning. This is what I think about when I think about fucking you. This is what it feels like when I'm jerking you off.

I tell you I am thinking about enrolling in courses. I say I want to start thinking about a degree. I go online and spend twenty minutes Googling myself before I lay down on the couch because of the heat.

I go online again later and see that you have been placing ads using my feet. There is an email in your inbox and when we go to dinner later I have to admit that I know your password and then I have to start over by apologizing before I ask you again about using my picture to save us a place at a party for swingers.

I have always wanted to cause a scene.

I take up my wine glass but then decide to drink it. I pick up your dinner as if to press it in your face, but then you get up and run out of the dining room and when I see you later you are walking along the road so I stop for you and take you with me.

METRO-GOLDWYN-MAYER
PRESENTS

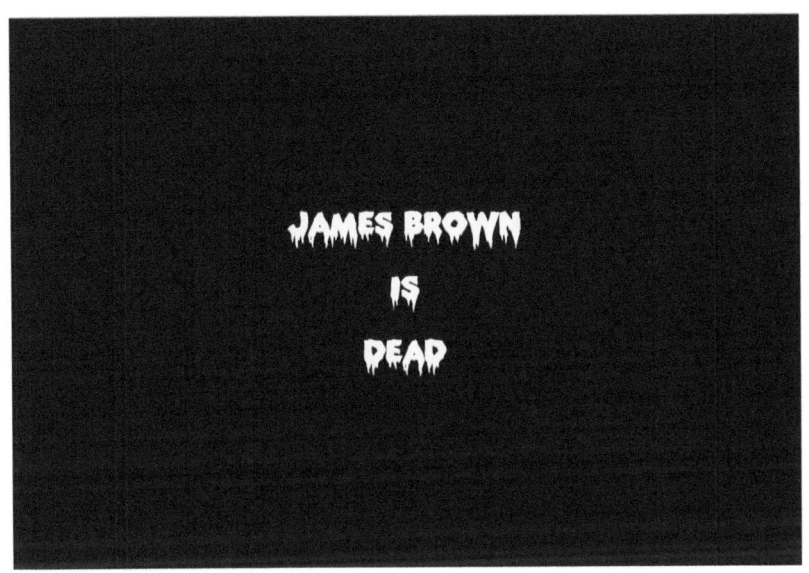

OR

JAMES BROWN IS OTHERWISE

COURTING THE ROSTER

OF THE AFTERLIFE

OR

SOME OTHER BRASH EXPLANATION

BY SYLVIA PLATH

STARRING RYAN GOSLING

BASED ON

A REMAKE OF THE INTERNET

DIRECTED BY CLINT EASTWOOD AND

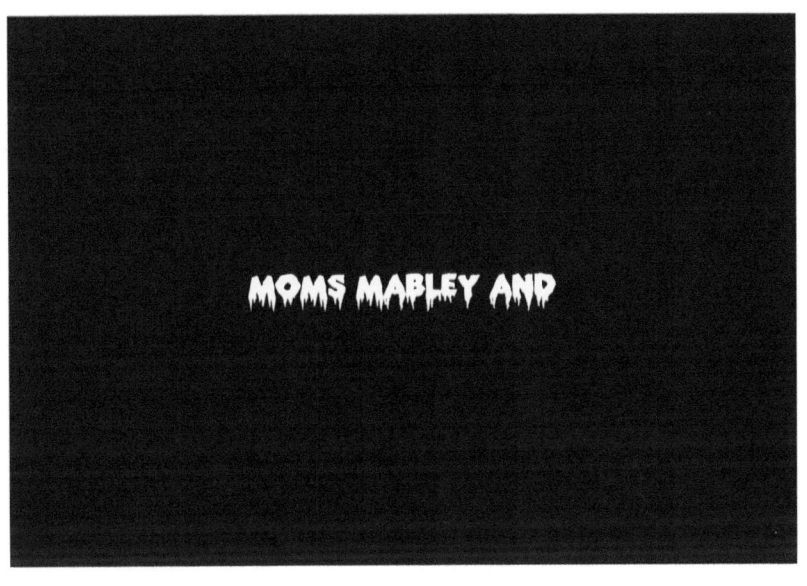

MOMS MABLEY AND

THE ESTATE OF HOWARD COSELL

DINO
DELAURENTIS
PRESENTS

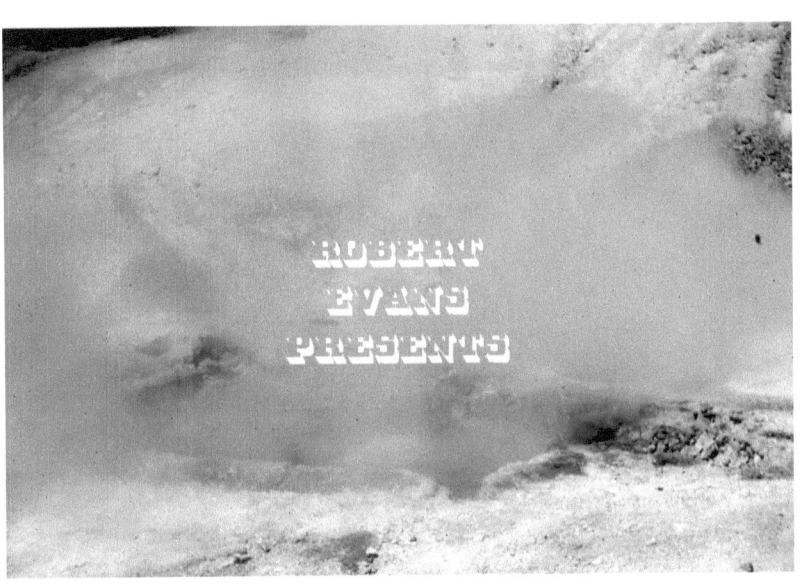

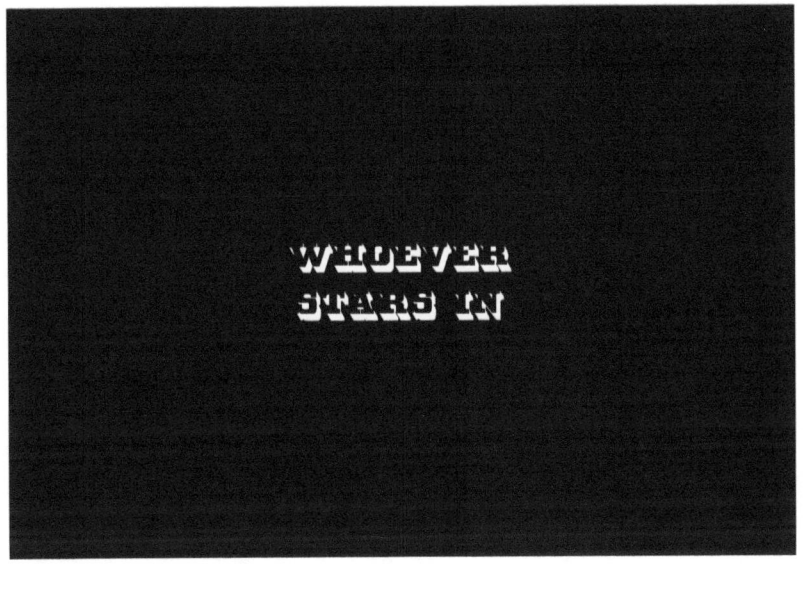

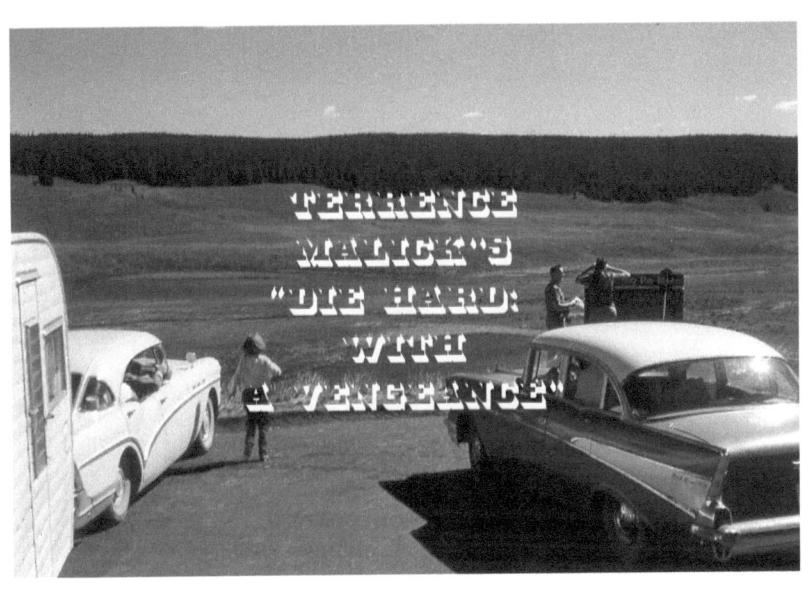

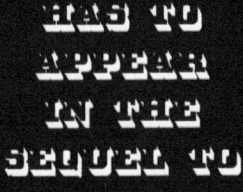

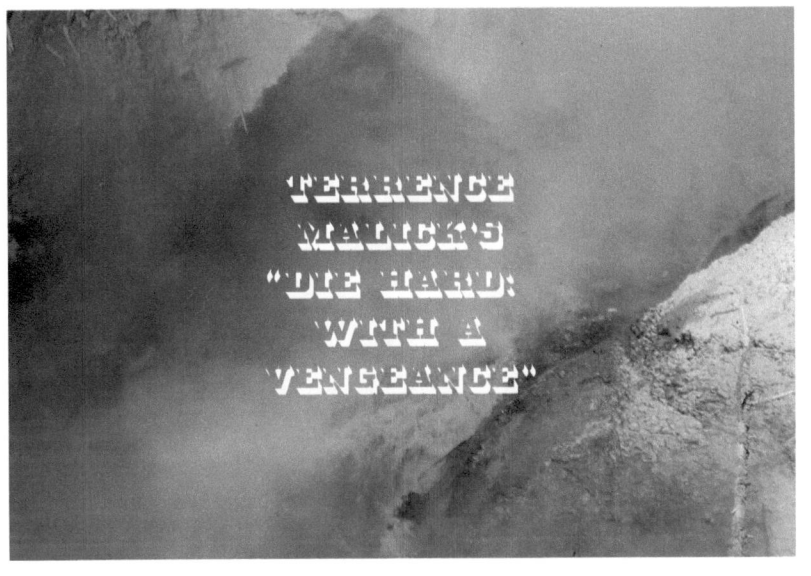

TERRENCE
MALICK'S
"DIE HARD:
WITH A
VENGEANCE"

AND CONSUME
THEIR HOUSE
IN TIRES
AND GO TO
THE POLICE.
IT'S JUST
AS USEFUL

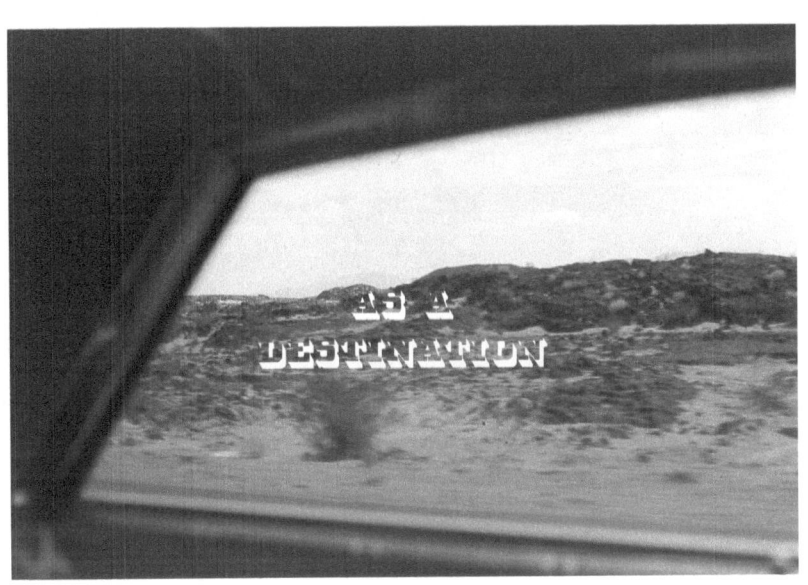

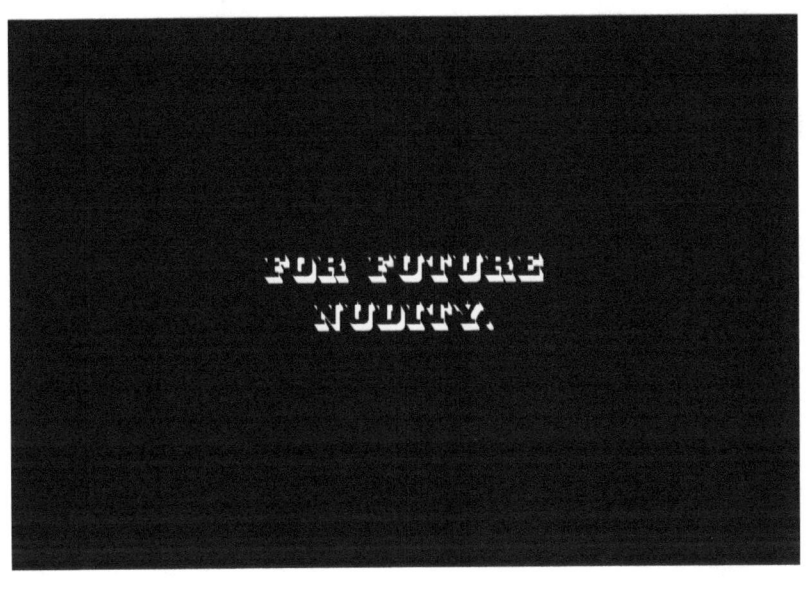

in D.W. Griffith's

"Way Down East"

Co-starring

Burr McIntosh

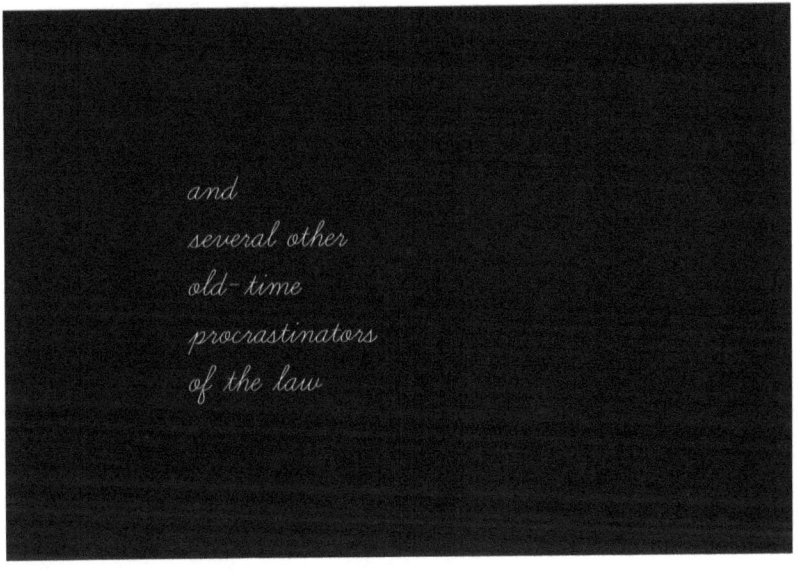

and
several other
old-time
procrastinators
of the law

Introducing
A Sudden
Blanket of Fog

and

Awkward Silence

by D.W. Griffith

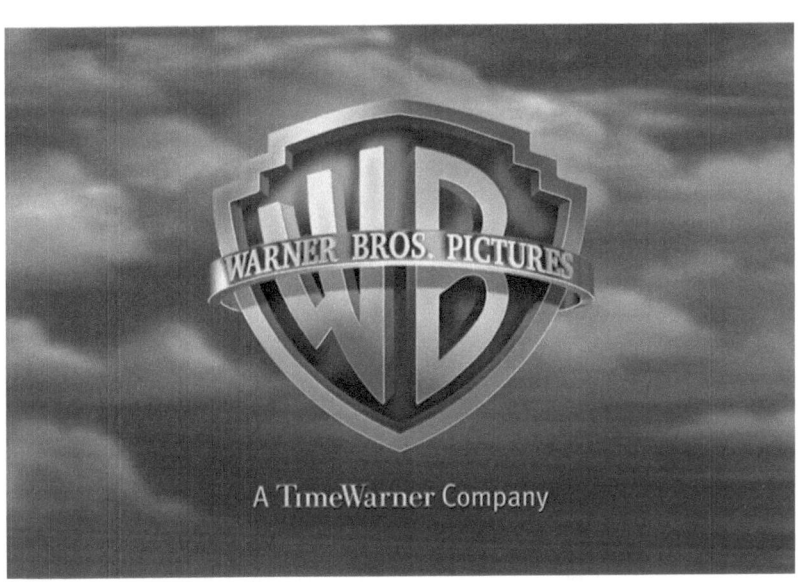

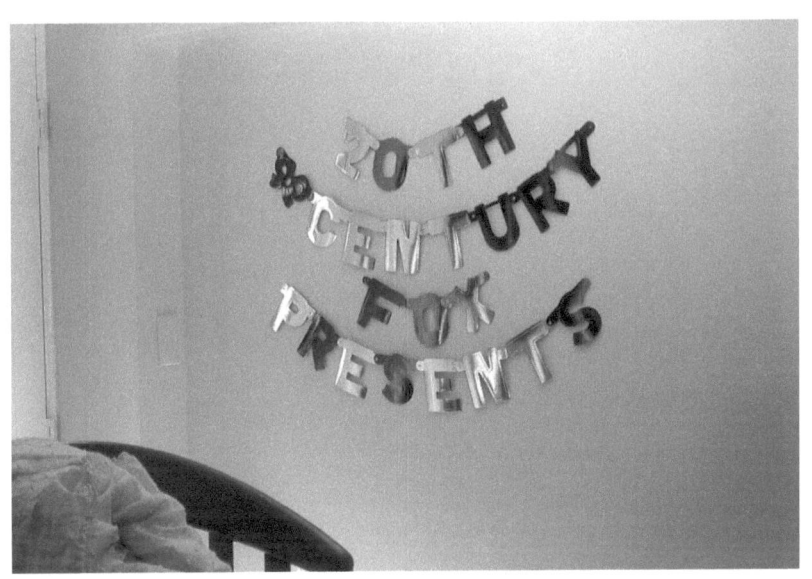

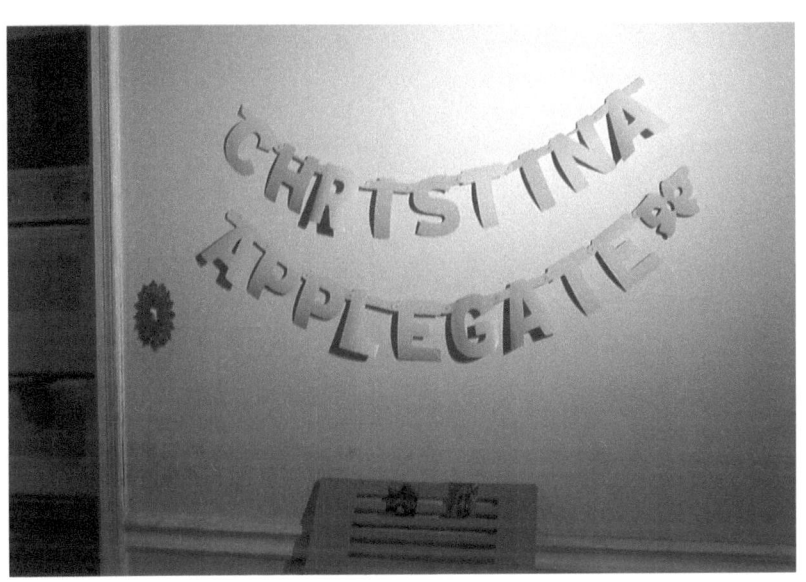

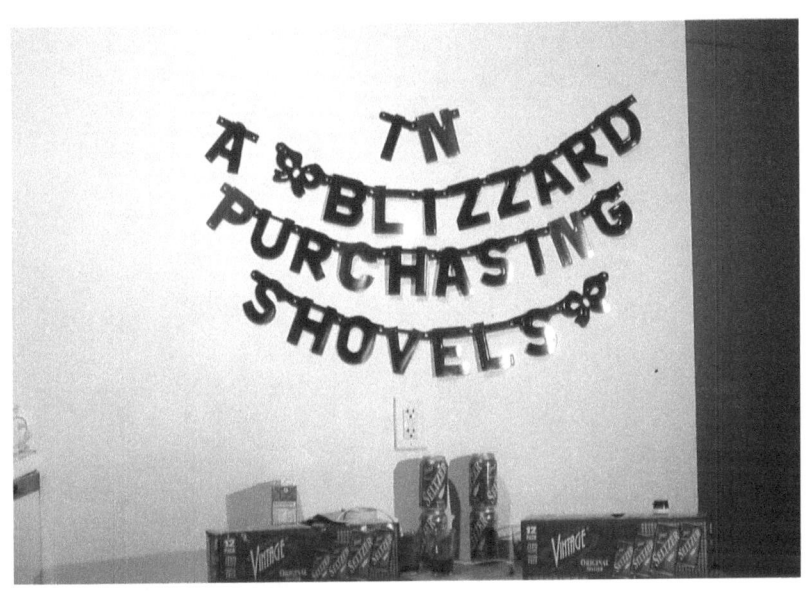

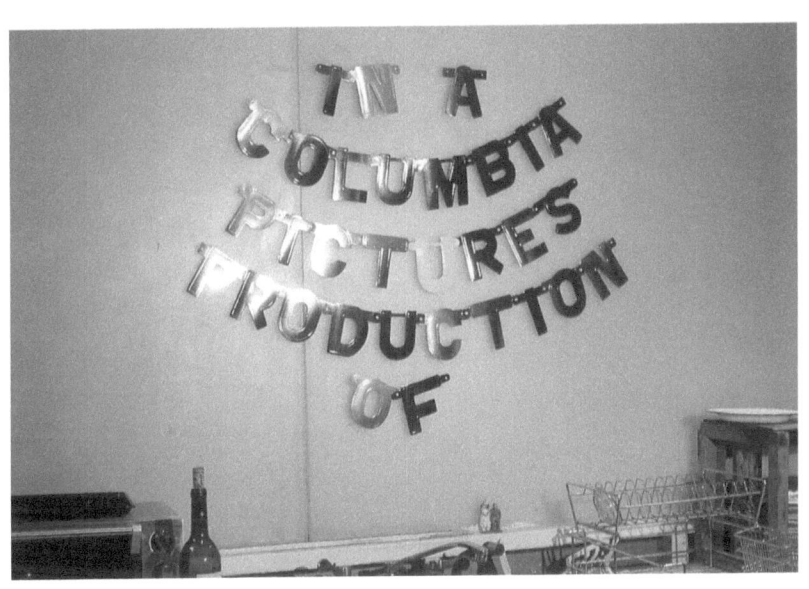

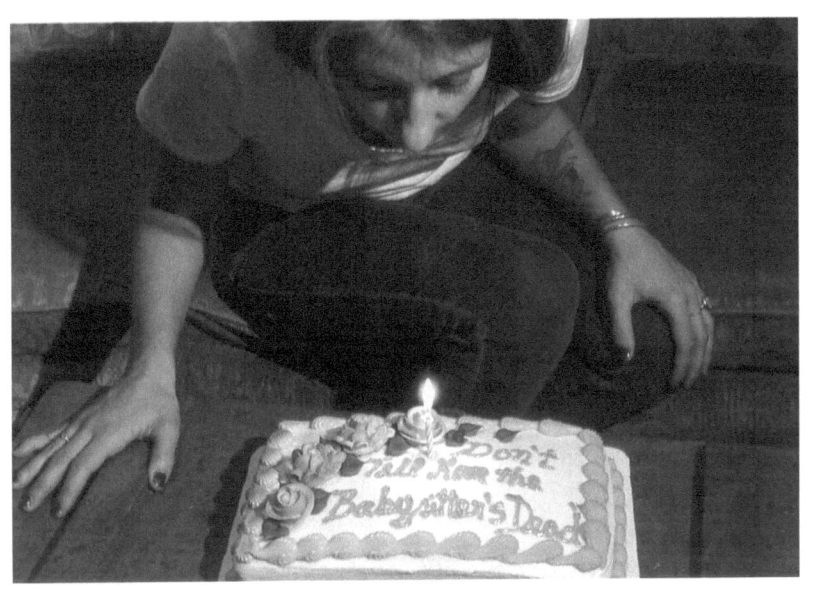

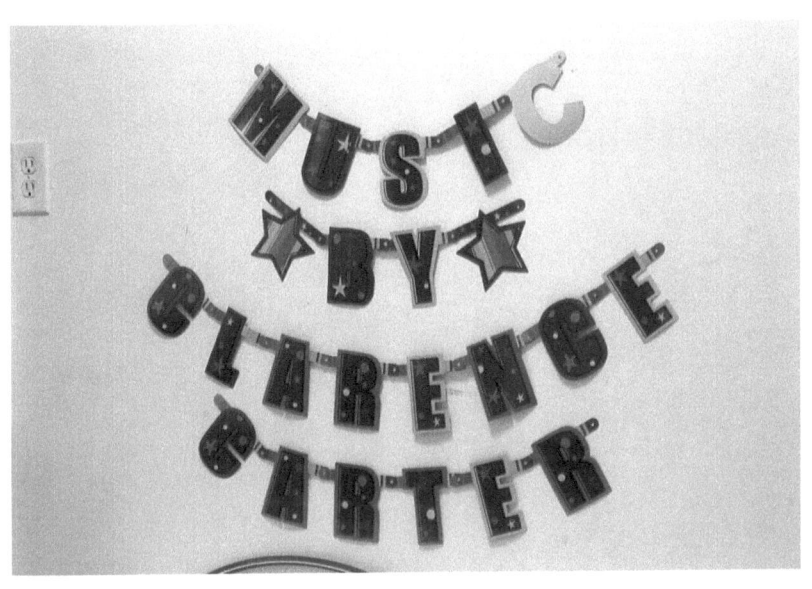

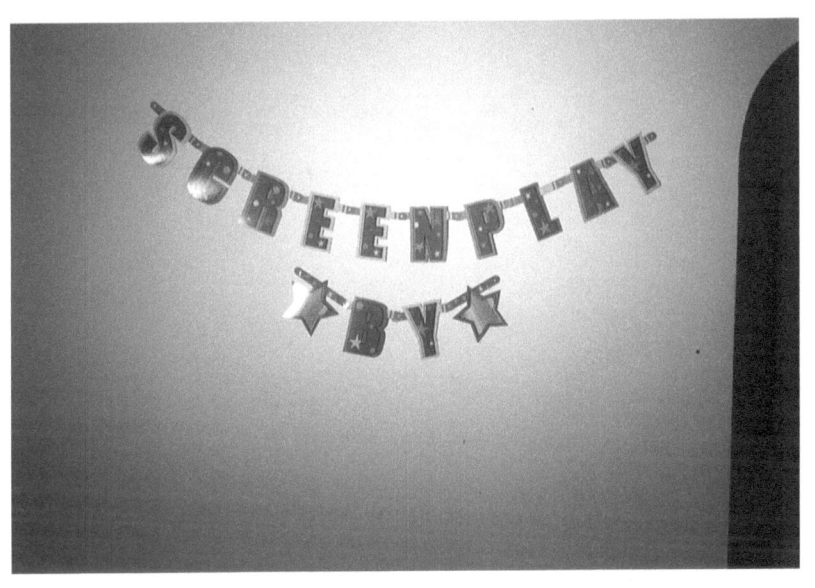

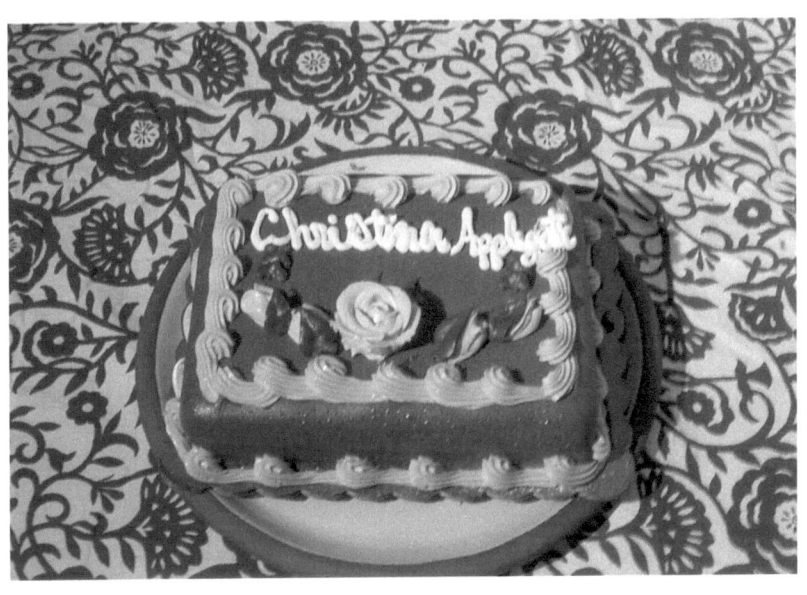

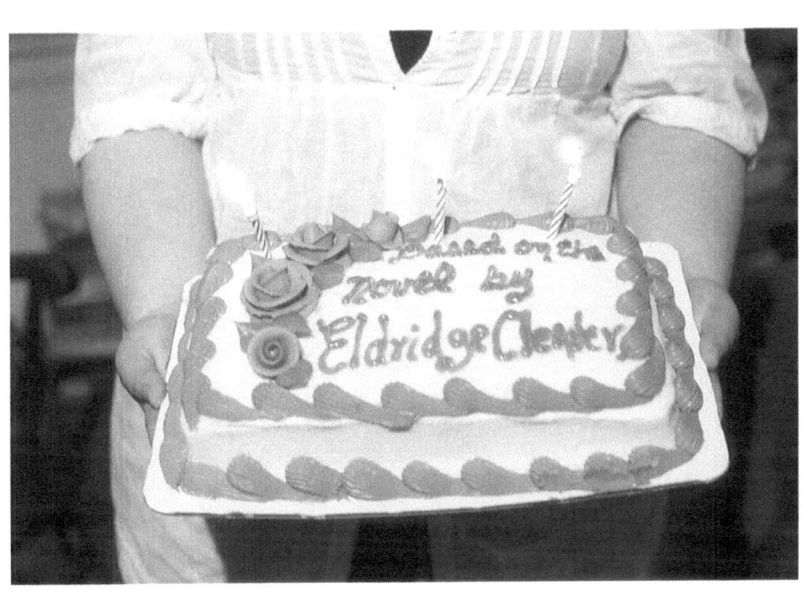

We don't
need another hero

going the distance
speaking French.

We were never there

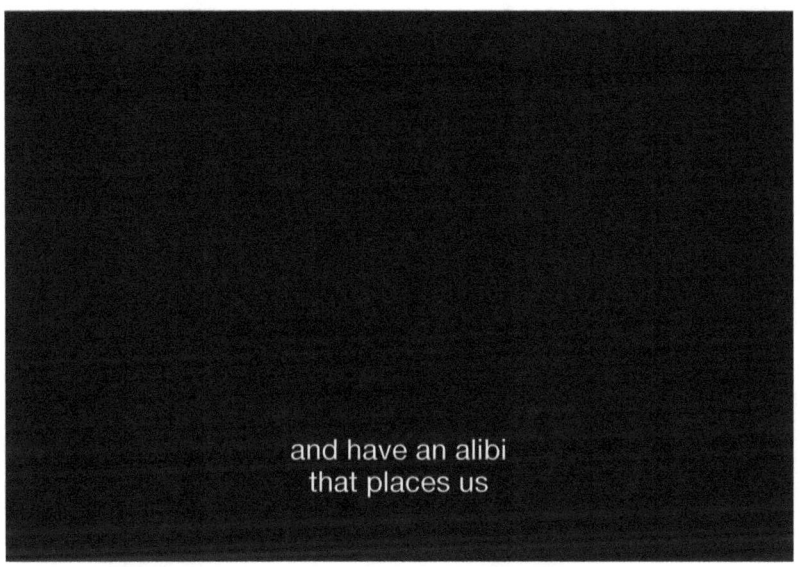

and have an alibi
that places us

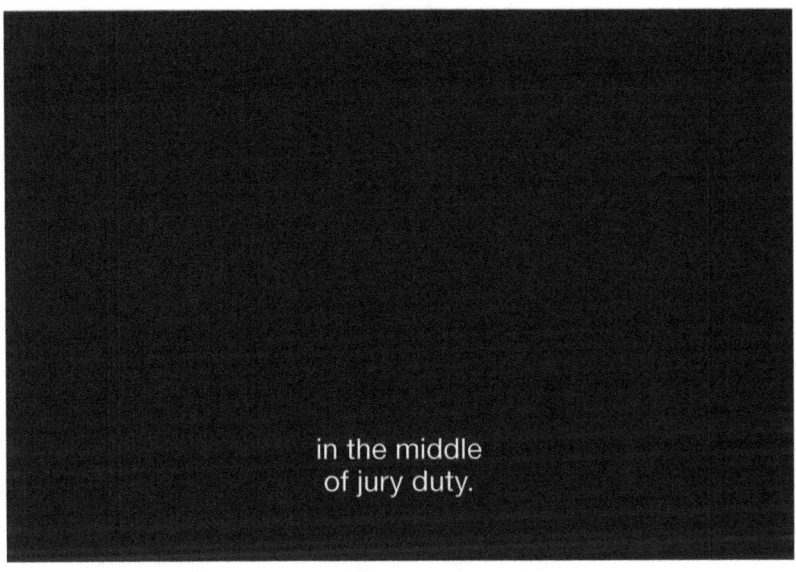

in the middle
of jury duty.

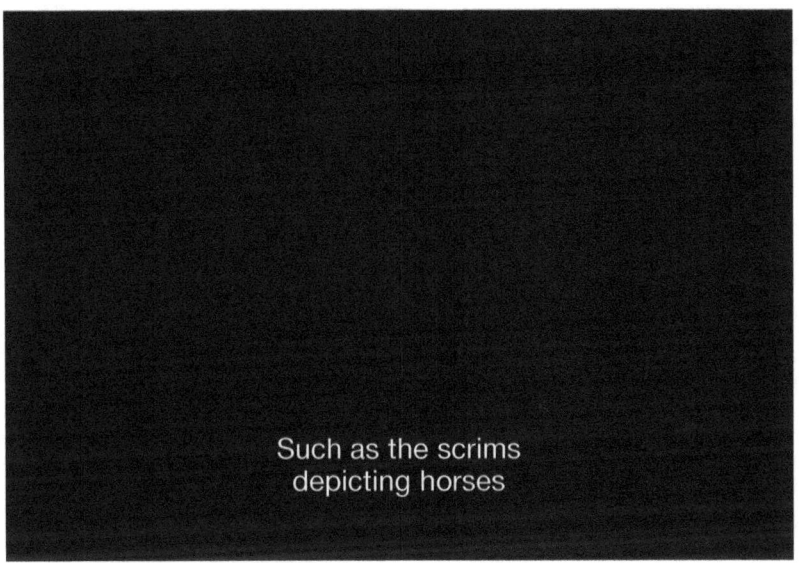

Such as the scrims
depicting horses

have dissolved
I am coming

in the night
to confess my love

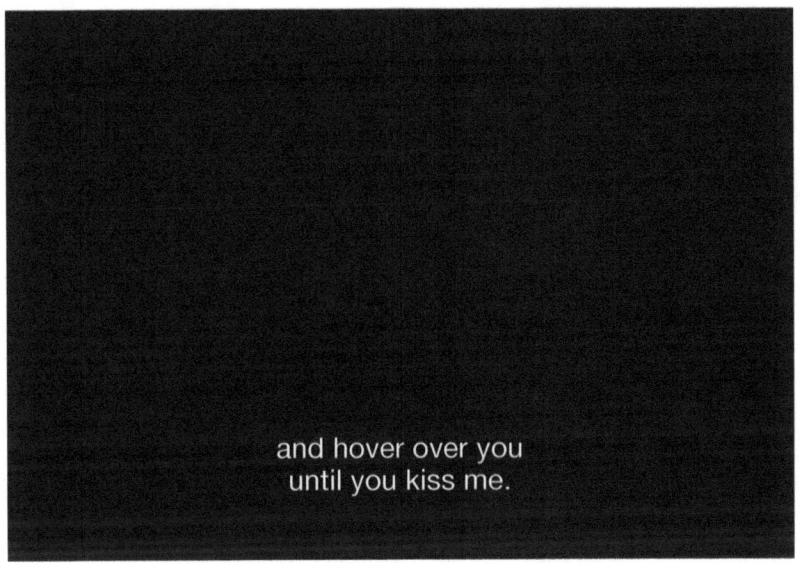

and hover over you
until you kiss me.

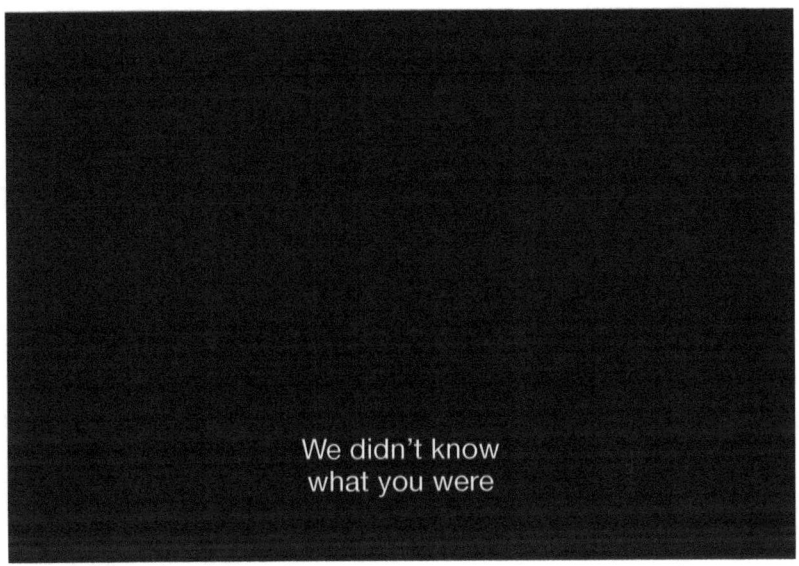

We didn't know
what you were

planning to respond
so we came over

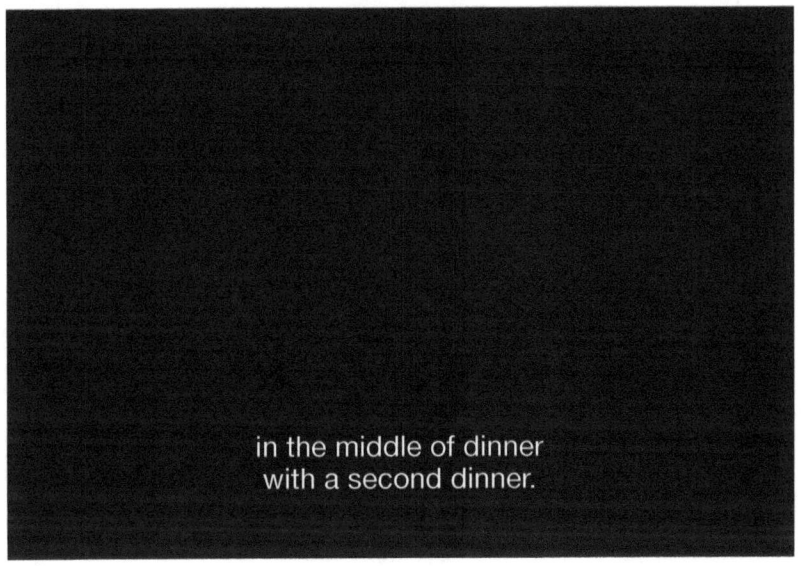

in the middle of dinner
with a second dinner.

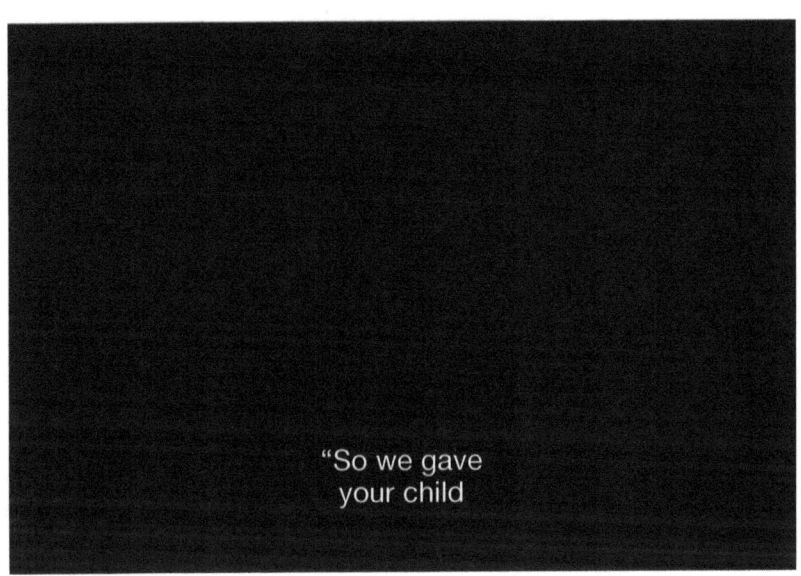

"So we gave
your child

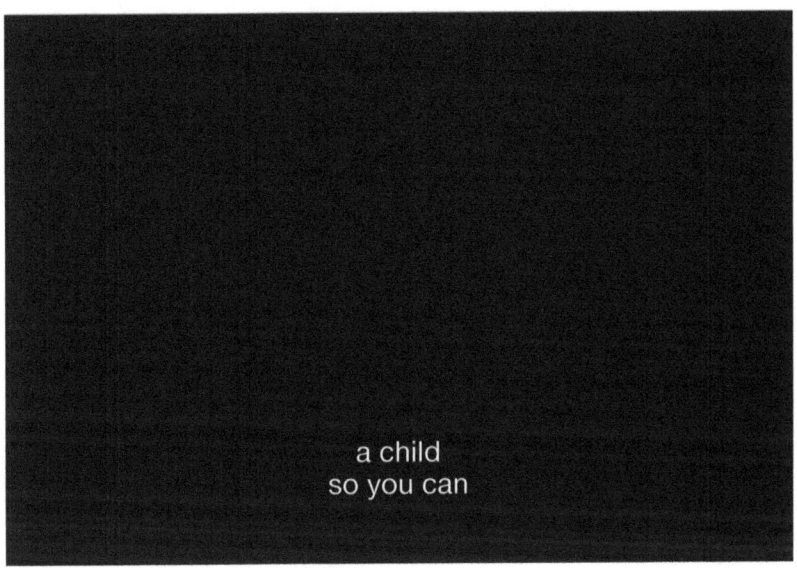

a child
so you can

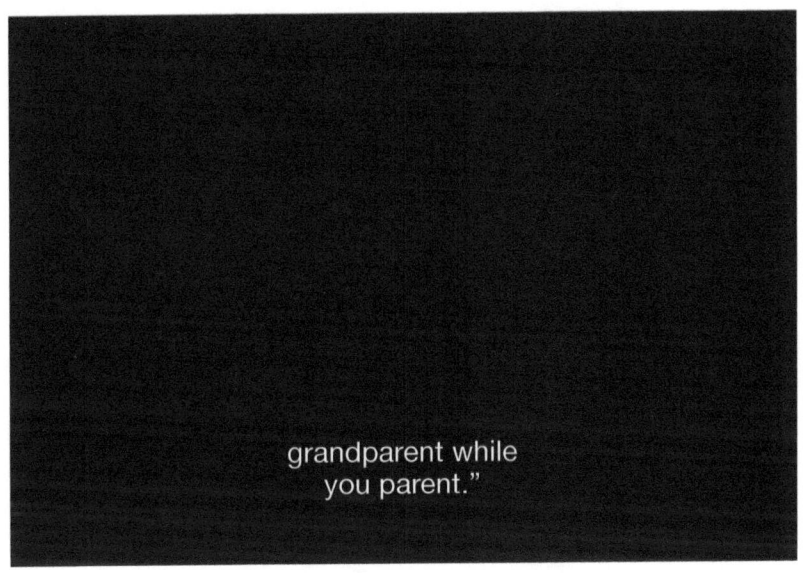

grandparent while
you parent."

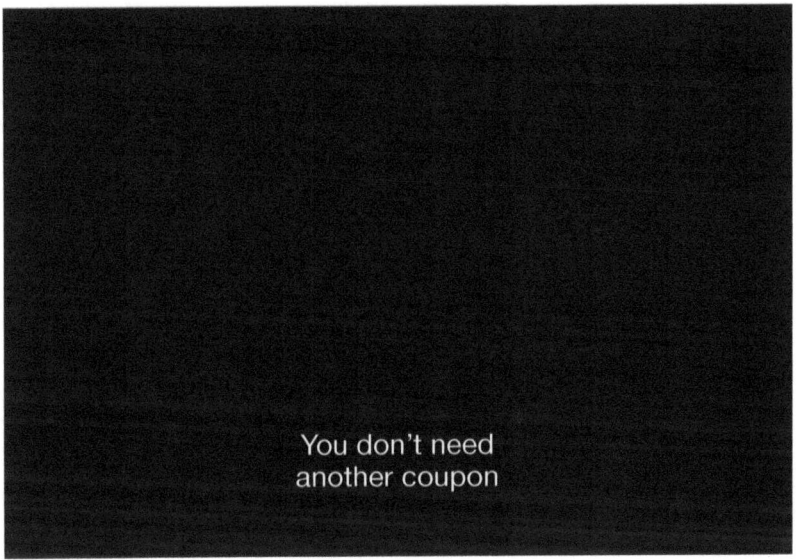

You don't need
another coupon

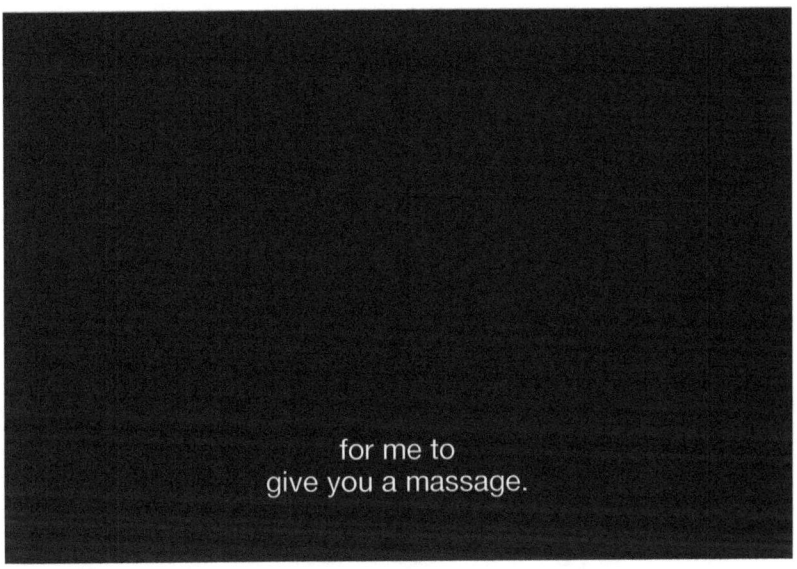

for me to
give you a massage.

The title of "James Brown is Dead" is borrowed from the painting, "James Brown is Dead" by Mark Bradford.

"We don't need another hero" is quoted from Tina Turner.

Thanks to: Steffani Jemison for putting up with the endless delays, to say nothing of her tirelessness and vision.

And Eric Sosnoff, Markisha Berrien and the Lower Manhattan Cultural Council for the time, space and resource materials necessary in making this book.

James Brown is Dead
Copyright © 2011 *Jibade-Khalil Huffman*

ISBN: 978-0-9833815-3-2

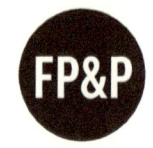

future plan and program

Future Plan and Program
http://futureplanandprogram.com

Please direct inquiries to:
thefuture@futureplanandprogram.com

Series editor: Steffani Jemison
Series designer: Sebastian Civarolo

Future Plan and Program was incubated in 2010-2011 by Project Row Houses.

Acknowledgements: Danielle Burns, Justin Cavin, Aisen Chacin, Ashley Clemmer-Hoffman, Cheryl Flores, Quincy Flowers, Hannah Ireland, Philip Jemison, Steven Jemison, Rick Lowe, Jasmine Jamillah Mahmoud, Phyllis McCallum, Solkem N'Gangbet, Michael Peranteau, Nikki Pressley, Linda Shearer, Martine Syms, Michael Kahlil Taylor, and Julie Thomson.

Future Plan and Program was generously funded in part by the following individuals: Kerry Inman & Denby Auble, John Roberson & John Blackmon, Danielle Antoinette Burns, Justin Cavin, Jereann Chaney, Melody Clark, Ashley Clemmer Hoffman & Brendan Hoffman, Phyllis L. McCallum and Steven Jemison, Joey Romano & Nicole Laurent, Victoria Thomas McGhee, Scott Sawyer & Michael Peranteau, Gregory & Diane Schultz, Leigh & Reggie Smith, and Rebecca Trahan. Special thanks to Jill Whitten & Robert Proctor.

Funding for Steffani Jemison's residency at Project Row Houses was provided by: The National Endowment for the Arts, the City of Houston through the Houston Arts Alliance, Houston Endowment Inc., The Brown Foundation, The Kresge Foundation, The Andy Warhol Foundation for the Visual Arts, and the Texas Commission on the Arts. Steffani Jemison's residency was part of a collaboration with the Core Program at the Glassell School of Art of the Museum of Fine Arts Houston.

www.ingramcontent.com/pod-product-compliance
Lightning Source LLC
Chambersburg PA
CBHW031123180526
45160CB00001B/2